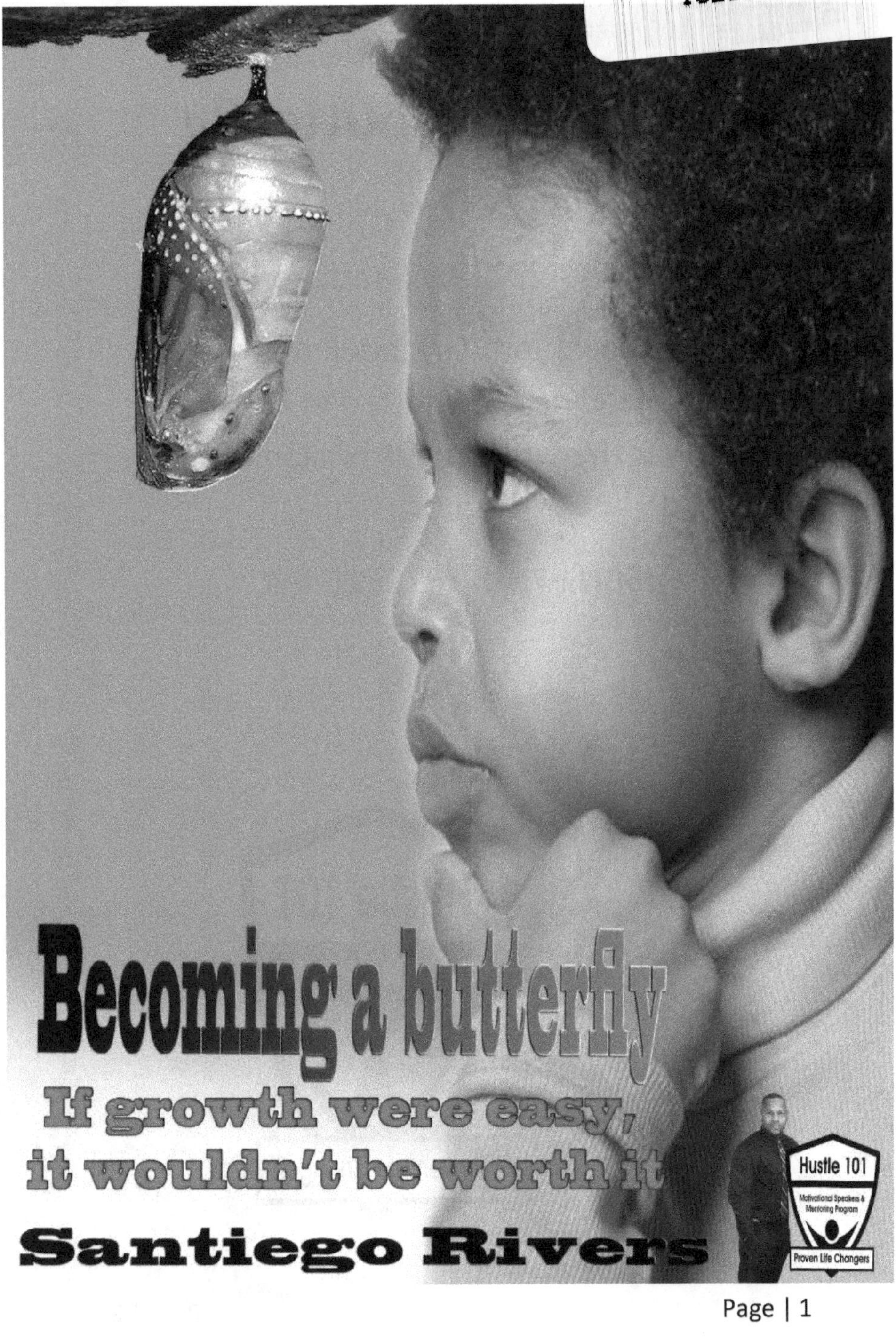
Becoming a butterfly
If growth were easy,
it wouldn't be worth it
Santiego Rivers
Hustle 101
Motivational Speakers & Mentoring Program
Proven Life Changers

Becoming a butterfly

(if growth were easy, it wouldn't be worth it)

Copyright © 2021 by **Santiego Rivers**

All rights reserved. This book may not be reproduced or transmitted in any form without the written permission of the author.

ISBN 978-1-7370516-6-4

Table of Content

Thoughts of the writer (pgs. 4-8)

Stage one: Discovering your purpose (pgs. 9-11)

Stage two: The application of faith and hard work (pgs. 12-13)

Stage three: The place where all journeys begin (pgs. 14-16)

Stage four: The by-product of your faith and hard work (pgs. 17-19)

The Final Affirmation (pgs. 20-23)

If you are fortunate to live long enough, life will present you with many different obstacles that will challenge you to grow, adapt, but, most of all, change.

The thinking process of the past and your fears about tomorrow will never solve today's problems or help you achieve the dreams of tomorrow.

The person you used to be will never deal with the issues you are currently facing and will see in the future.

You can't spend your whole life running. Even Forrest Gump had to learn to slow down and face life head-on. So, it would be best if you discovered a reason to plant your feet and fight because the only certainty in life is change.

Are you willing to fight for the change that you desire?

Will the transformation you encounter highlight your growth, or will the change reveal what other people think about you and your chances at achieving success?

(You are not prepared to face the challenge ahead)

Only your hard work can answer that question honestly.

A wise man knows and understands the meaning of the following quote;

> *"Perfection is highlighted by all the imperfections that surround it."*

My question to you is, what will your scars, flaws, and fears tell me about the process that you had to endure to discover your perfection?

As a youth and even in my adult years, I have faced tests and fears that left me in tears.

The mental and physical abuse from the outside allowed my soul to think that it was okay.

I remember when other people called me stupid and ugly so many times that I believed that I was. I held onto every unkind word said to me like a badge of honor.

It would take me many years to learn that you don't have to answer or respond to the words or the names that other people call you.

Knowledge has blessed me with the following understanding that I pray reaches those people who need to be inspired or simply change:

(Hurt people hurt other people)

There is no honor in tearing someone down if you are not willing to build them up.

It takes more strength and courage to build somebody up than to tear them down, either mentally or physically, because you have insecurities that you are running from.

How do larvae become a butterfly? How does a creature who could barely move on earth learn to fly in the sky?

Don't the larvae know from birth that their life would not amount to much? So how could their life amount to anything, right?

The stages that the larvae go through to become the best version of themselves are the same process that we must commit to achieving ourselves.

For many of us, our life resembles the larvae. We are born into a world that does not foster or encourage our growth.

Unlike the larvae, we get caught in one stage of our life. Then, because of our fears and insecurities, we don't move on.

Stage One

We are born into a world trying to figure out where we belong and how we plan to get there.

Not knowing the path to our future, we are stuck depending on the people around us for guidance. What happens when that guidance leaves us more confused about our future before we began to think about our future?

Who do the larvae tell about their plans to fly in the sky one day? But, of course, the insects around the larvae will never fly, so how could they ever comprehend the destiny of the larvae?

All the other insects do is try to put doubt inside the mind of the larvae?

Who are you to be great when I am not great?

That is the actual feeling of the small-minded people that you tell your big dreams too.

Never expect someone else to see or understand your vivid dreams when they are stuck with their black and white images and their uncertainty about their future.

Stage one is where we begin to look for help and support in starting on our path.

There are those people who are lucky enough to find guidance on their path, but for many others, they must figure things out on their own.

Many people get stuck in **stage one** of their journey because the path is not clear, and the doubts of others have become the loudest thoughts in their minds.

What will the larvae do in this situation? Do they still desire to become a butterfly despite what everyone else says?

The larvae will simply move onto **stage two** of their journey to fly in the sky.

Stage Two

Stage two is where you decide to block out other people's doubts and only listen to the voice within your soul that knows that you can do what other people think is impossible.

Somewhere within, you know that what everyone else thinks are impossible becomes possible when someone finally does it.

You decide to look in the mirror and ask yourself the following question:

Why not you?

The most challenging questions always have a simple answer. You must get to a point in your life where you ask yourself the right question to inspire you to believe in yourself.

To achieve the impossible, you must make it possible. So, during **stage two** of your journey, you start doing all the things it will take to get you to the next stage.

The larvae begin to eat everything in sight so that they can become a caterpillar. In this stage, we must become dedicated students/pupils.

We must learn everything that we need to know to guide us on our journey. Talent without hard work is useless. Therefore, *stage two* will require you to work hard despite the skills that you may possess.

A person with talent will always find it challenging to defeat a foe willing to work hard to achieve their goals.

Stage Three

During **stage three**, you will be at the most challenging stage that you will face on your journey.

This stage is the most difficult because it will require you to apply all the skills that helped you complete the other steps thus far.

Stage one required you to learn to believe in yourself when the people around you tried to fill your mind with doubt.

In **stage two**, you had to learn how to apply hard work & faith to the talent that you already possessed.

In **stage two**, you applied discipline, dedication, late nights, and commitment to your craft to push you in ways that amazed even yourself.

While you are in **stage three**, you will begin to search within yourself to motivate yourself to face the final stage you will be completing.

The caterpillar goes into its cocoon during this stage to face the most formidable foe they will ever encounter.

If there is no enemy within, the enemy on the outside can do no harm.

During **stage three**, the only opinion that matters is yours. Will you win, or will you lose.

The answer became clear when you decided to make it this far on your journey. As you complete this stage, you will show the people who doubted you and did not believe the big dreams you shared with them were possible.

You are now working hard in the dark so that in **stage four**, you will shine in the light.

Stage Four

In **stage four**, you will show everyone who doubted you along the way what your faith and hard work have produced.

You struggled through the different stages, overcoming ridicule and doubt from other people, which at times made those feelings yours.

You persevered through everything that the world put in your path to make you stray off your course.

Your **faith** made you believe even when the road ahead was unclear. Your **hard work** made you apply the effort you needed to bite down on your teeth and accomplish feats that other people felt were impossible.

You made the impossible possible by believing in yourself and not giving up on your dreams.

The larvae become a butterfly by not giving up on their dreams. No, the path to becoming a butterfly for the larvae is not easy, but it proves that all the struggles it endured as it flies in the sky were worth it.

What dream or desire that you hold within do you desire to have manifest in your life? What fears and doubts are you willing to replace with **faith** and **hard work** to prove the impossible?

The stages of our lives are like the chapters of our favorite book. We may encounter heartache, pain, and tears, but that does not mean that the next chapter will not become the thing we need to become successful.

Your success will be from the by-product of your **faith** and **hard work** that made you believe in something greater than yourself.

Imagine being born into a world that looks down on you because of your **circumstances**. Yet, despite the situation you face, your ability and determination to achieve your dreams will defy all the odds.

There is more to living than just being alive. Life should be lived and not just settling for what life brings your way.

Will life be hard? Will life be tough? Life will be whatever you decide to make it. Everyone will face some adversity in their lives.

It is never about the situations that we face in life. It is about how we respond to the problems in our lives that matters.

We must make it through the winter to appreciate the spring, the fall, and the summer.

Adversity and struggle will tell you more about yourself than success will ever reveal. No one who has not tasted defeat can ever tell you why victory is so rewarding.

To claim victory, you must be willing to stand on your words and deliver with your actions.

You can't be afraid to **F.A.I.L.** because your **F**irst **A**ttempt **In** **L**earning will not be your last attempt if you plan on succeeding.

Often victory comes one more attempt after you refused to quit. You know that it cost too much to fail, so you keep moving forward like the little engine that could.

You must be willing to throw your whole self at what you want to achieve out of life. Big dreams will require you to make enormous sacrifices.

What sacrifices are you willing to make?

The larvae's change to become a butterfly shows you what it is willing to do to fulfill its dreams.

What about you? What are you willing to do to fulfill your dreams and desires? No one can make you want something that you don't want to achieve for yourself.

One of the best inspirational quotes that I ever heard regarding learning to believe in yourself is the following:

"If you are not willing to learn, no one can help you. If you are determined to learn, no one can ever stop you."- **Zig Ziglar**

You must be willing to dare to be great, just for the opportunity to be successful. You must be willing to invest in yourself.

Your dreams are not impossible if you are willing to work to make them possible. Faith without work is dead

Would you please not allow your dreams to die because you were too afraid to try to give them life?

Your **faith** and **hard work** are the breath of life that will sustain you when the road ahead seems bleak and unsure. Trust the process. Trust yourself.

There is something in you that the enemy is trying to stop manifesting in your life. Would you mind not doing the enemy's work for them? Instead, dare to be great and apply the hard work needed to make your dreams come true.

www.ingramcontent.com/pod-product-compliance
Lightning Source LLC
Chambersburg PA
CBHW071014160426
43193CB00012B/2053